A PASTOR'S COUNSEL

A Pastor's Counsel

Words of Wisdom for Weary,
Wounded and Wandering Sheep

George Burder
J.W. Chickering
Philip Doddridge
Jonathan Edwards
Ashbel Green
Thomas Scott

Solid Ground Christian Books
Birmingham, Alabama USA

Solid Ground Christian Books
PO Box 660132
Vestavia Hills AL 35266
205-443-0311
sgcb@charter.net
www.solid-ground-books.com

A PASTOR'S COUNSEL
Words of Wisdom for Weary, Wounded & Wandering Sheep

George Burder (1752-1832)
J.W. Chickering (1831-1913)
Philip Doddridge (1702-1751)
Jonathan Edwards (1703-1758)
Ashbel Green (1762-1848)
Thomas Scott (1747-1821)

Taken from the *American Tract Society* edition of 1877

Cover image is taken from a photo by Ric Ergenbright
of sheep on a hillside in Devon, England.

Cover design by Borgo Design
Contact them at borgogirl@bellsouth.net

ISBN: 978-1-59925-157-8

TABLE OF CONTENTS

PUBLISHER'S INTRODUCTION

"The way of a fool is right in his own eyes,
But a wise man is he who listens to counsel."
(Proverbs 12:15)
"He who walks with wise men will be wise,
But the companion of fools will suffer harm."
(Proverbs 13:20)
"Listen to counsel and accept discipline,
That you may be wise the rest of your days."
(Proverbs 19:20)
"For by wise guidance you will wage war,
And in abundance of counselors there is victory."
(Proverbs 24:6)

These texts drawn from Proverbs serve as a fitting introduction to the little gem you hold in your hands. Those who wrote the brief articles that are now before you were some of the wisest and choicest servants of God this fallen world has known.

In John Bunyan's classic work *Pilgrim's Progress* the leading figure in the book, whose name is Christian, is led into a house that is called The House of the Interpreter. This House represents the ministry of the Holy Spirit to the new convert, and there are seven powerful lessons taught in this House. The very first lesson is the description of a true pastor, whom, we are told "is the only man whom the Lord of the place whither thou art going hath authorized to be thy guide in all difficult places thou mayest meet with in the way." What are the marks of a true pastor according to Bunyan? There are seven, which are found in these words:

> *Christian saw a picture of a very grave person hang up against the wall; and this was the fashion of it: it had eyes lifted up to heaven, the best of books in his hand, the law of truth was written upon his lips, the world was behind his back; he stood as if he pleaded with men, and a crown of gold didst hang over his head.*

First, the true pastor should be a man who is *grave*. The idea that is found in this word is that of being serious and solemn. This is well captured in the words of Richard Baxter, "I preached as never sure to preach again, and as a dying man to dying men." Sadly, in our day it is all too rare to find men who are serious, sober and solemn. Such were the men whose articles fill this book.

Second, the true pastor should be a man *with his eyes lifted up to heaven*. In the spirit of Samuel the pastor you trust should be able to say, "Moreover, as for me, far be it from me that I should sin against the LORD by ceasing to pray for you..." (1 Samuel 12:23). The man you trust must above all be known as a man of prayer.

Third, the true pastor should be a man *with the best of books in his hand*. In the spirit of the Psalmist your earthly shepherd should be able to say, "O how I love Your law! It is my meditation all the day" (Psalm 119:97). While all ministers of the gospel should be reading the best Christian books available, he must be devoted to the Bible as the word of the living God. Trust no man who does not trust the Bible.

Fourth, the true pastor should be a man *with the law of truth written upon his lips*. In the language of the prophet Malachi, "The law of truth was in his mouth, and injustice was not found on his lips. He walked with Me in peace and equity, and turned many away from iniquity" (Malachi 2:6). It is not enough that a man carries his Bible in his hand, he must have it written within his heart, and coming out from his lips.

Fifth, the true pastor should be a man *with the world behind his back.* A worldly minister is a contradiction of terms. "Love not the world, neither the things that are in the world. If any man love the world, the love of the Father is not in him" (1 John 2:15). The Apostle Paul was able to say, "But God forbid that I should glory, save in the cross of our Lord Jesus Christ, by whom the world is crucified unto me, and I unto the world" (Galatians 6:14). One of the marks of a false teacher, according to Thomas Brooks, is "They eye your goods more than your good; and mind more the serving of themselves, than the saving of your souls. So they may have your substance, they care not though Satan has your souls (Revelation 18:11-13)."

Sixth, the true pastor should be a man *who pleads with men.* In the language of the Lord through Ezekiel, "And I will bring you into the wilderness of the people, and there will I plead with you face to face. Like as I pleaded with your fathers in the wilderness of the land of Egypt, so will I plead with you, saith the Lord GOD." (Ezekiel 20:35,36). All who represent our Lord Jesus Christ must be like the Apostle Peter of whom we are told, "And with many other words he solemnly testified and kept on exhorting them, saying, 'Be saved from this perverse generation!'" (Acts 2:40). And he must be like the Apostle Paul, who is described in Athens, "Now while Paul waited for them at Athens, his spirit was provoked within him when he saw that the city was given over to idols. Therefore he reasoned in the synagogue with the Jews and with the *Gentile* worshipers, and in the marketplace daily with those who happened to be there" (Acts 17:16,17). The men who wrote the chapters in this little book were all known by their earnest desire to see souls saved.

Finally, the true pastor should be a man *with a crown of gold above his head.* In the language of Bunyan, "that is to show thee, that slighting and despising the things that are present, for the love that he hath to his Master's service, he is sure in the world that comes next to have glory for his reward." It is a tragedy that multitudes of modern day pastors drive the finest cars, eat the finest food, wear the finest clothes and live in the finest homes. Do not permit such a man to be your guide in the difficult places you are sure to meet with in the way to the heavenly city. Seek a shepherd after God's own heart, who has his eyes fixed upon the world to come.

As you prepare to read this book called *A Pastor's Counsel,* pause first and pray for eyes to see, ears to hear, and a heart to feel the weight of the truth set before you. Do not be in a hurry. Take your time and let each truth settle down within your heart. Heed the words of the Apostle Paul, "But examine everything carefully; hold fast to that which is good" (1 Thessalonians 5:21). May you find in these pages the wisdom that is from above, and upon embracing them for yourself seek to pass them on to others, for our Lord Jesus said, "It is more blessed to give than to receive" (Acts 20:35).

The Publisher

A
PASTOR'S COUNSEL

WHAT IS IT TO BELIEVE
ON CHRIST?

I WILL suppose that you have at some time felt alarmed in view of your sins, and inquired in your thoughts, if not in words, "What must I do to be saved?" You have the same answer that Paul gave to the jailer, "Believe on the Lord Jesus Christ." Still you hesitate. You ask what this language means. You desire to know *what it is* to believe on Christ.

Your wish, fellow-sinner, is a very reasonable one. The wonder and the sin is, that you have not asked such a question before. It is a most important

and solemn question. It has much to do
with your salvation : for the BIBLE declares, "He that believeth on the SON
hath everlasting life ; and he that believeth not the SON, shall not see life ; *but the
wrath of* GOD *abideth on him.*"

"*What is it to believe on Christ?*" It is,

TO FEEL YOUR NEED OF HIM ;

TO BELIEVE THAT HE IS ABLE AND WILL-
ING TO SAVE YOU, AND TO SAVE YOU NOW;
and

TO CAST YOURSELF UNRESERVEDLY ON
HIS MERCY, and TRUST IN HIM ALONE FOR
SALVATION.

To feel your need of him. Till you do
this, you will never seek him earnestly,
or trust him wholly. You do not send
for a physician till you feel yourself to
be ill. It was only when Peter found he
was beginning to sink, that he cried,
"Lord, save me." So the sinner never
goes to Christ in a right manner, till he
feels himself to be a lost, wretched be-

ing. It is not enough to *know* this: you must *feel* it.

Do you say *you cannot?* O, then, *how* lost, *how* wretched you must be! Your very language ought to fill you with shame and fear. Whose fault is it that you do not feel? How long need it be before you feel? You can feel *alarm* when a murderer holds you in his grasp; you can feel *sorrow* when a friend is dying in agony before your eyes; and can you feel no sorrow when you think of a suffering Saviour, whose love you have abused—no alarm, when you call to mind that fearful judgment to which you are hastening? Will you dare tell your Judge, at the great day, that you could not feel your need of a Saviour?

But you say, "I *do* feel, at least in some degree, that I am a poor, guilty, undone sinner; but this will not save me." *No,* *it will not.* Thousands have felt this and perished. You must also

Believe that Christ is able and willing to save you, and to save you NOW. He is able, for he is almighty. You are a great sinner, but Christ is a great Saviour. Satan has been trying to persuade you that Christ is not able to save so great a sinner as you are. It is false. He *is* able; and unless you *believe this* in all its glorious extent, you will no more be willing to trust him, than a man on the roof of a burning house will step upon a weak ladder which he knows will give way beneath him.

You must believe that he is *willing.* He has in many ways shown himself to be willing. If you doubt it, you disbelieve and offend him. Does it please him, think you, when he utters this kind welcome, " WHOSOEVER cometh unto me, *I will in no wise cast out,*" to hear you reply, " O Lord, I cannot think that thou wouldst receive such a one as me, if I *should* come ?" Yet you do in effect say this every moment you cherish the feeling that you are too sinful to hope for pardon. You mistake this for humility; but it is unbelief and sin.

You must believe that he is willing *now*. Perhaps you have thought he *would* be willing, after a few more days or weeks spent in praying and weeping and growing better. Be assured your worst enemy wants no more than that you should continue to think so. *You are growing no better.* You are doing nothing to gain Christ's favor while you refuse to yield to his invitations. Until you believe that he is able and willing to save you, and to do it NOW, you never will be saved. The great enemy of your soul does not wish you to set a time *far distant* when you can go to Christ, and when he will be willing to receive you. If you will *continue* to place that time at the distance of a week, or an hour, or a minute, his object is gained, and your soul is lost.

But you ask, "Does not a sinner, at the moment of his actual submission to the Saviour, feel more fit to be pardoned; and is not Christ more willing to pardon him than ever before?" No, dear friend, NO. He was *less* fit to be pardoned, for his sins had been increasing every moment up to that very time; and Christ was no more *willing* to pardon him than he had always been. Every Christian will tell you that so far as Christ's willingness was concerned, he might as well have found peace in him months or years sooner, as when he hopes he *was* pardoned. The next thing required of you is,

To cast yourself unreservedly upon his mercy, and trust in him alone for salvation. This implies that you renounce all expectations of saving yourself, or of being saved any other way than through the righteousness and redemption of Christ. Did you ever feel as if you had done all you could? Have you tried to think of something more to do, to obtain hope and forgiveness? You have done *too much* in this way already.

Just stop doing, and begin to trust Christ to do all, and you are safe. A man is rowing a boat on a river just above a dreadful cataract. The current begins to bear him downward, the spectators on the banks give him up for lost; " He is gone," they all exclaim. But in another moment a rope is thrown towards the wretched man, it strikes the water near the boat; *now* how does the case stand? Do all the spectators call upon him *to row*, to row *stronger*, to *try harder* to reach the shore, when with every stroke of his arm the boat is evidently floating towards the falls? O no, the eager and united cry is, "*Drop your oars! Give up your desperate attempt!* TAKE HOLD OF THE ROPE!" But he chooses to row, and in a few minutes he disappears and perishes. All his hope lay not in row-

ing, but in *ceasing* to row; for while he
was rowing he could not grasp the rope.
So all the sinner's hope lies not in strug-
gling to save himself, but in *ceasing* to
struggle; for while he expects soon to
accomplish the work of salvation, he will
not look to Christ to do it for him. It is
not *doing*, but *yielding*, that is required.

But you say, "If all I have to do is to
cease from attempting to save myself, and
to be willing that Christ should do the
work of my salvation, why do you urge
me *to become a Christian*, or to do *any
thing*? Why not let me sit still, and wait
till Christ shall come and pardon me?"
And what if the man in the boat had
dropped his oar, and then folded his
hands and waited for the rope to save
him? He might as well have died rowing as sitting still, and would *as certainly*
have died in the latter case as in the for-
mer. But he must *grasp the rope*. So
the sinner must *lay hold upon the cross—*

not by waiting till he is better, but by
first concluding that he shall never be
any better in the way he is going on, and
then *looking to Christ.* As he perceives
the ground sinking beneath him, and feels
how lost and wretched he is, filled with
mingled despair and hope—despair in
himself, and hope in the power and mercy of Christ—he says,

> " I stand upon a mountain's edge,
>   O save me, lest I fall."

His prayer is heard—the heart of the compassionate Saviour is ready to welcome
him—the arms of mercy are stretched
out to receive him—a word of kind welcome reaches his ear, " *Son be of good
cheer; thy sins be forgiven thee.*" He be-
lieves that word—he trusts that heart—
he falls into those arms, *and he is safe.*

Now, dear reader, your question is
answered. Is not the answer true? Is
it not *plain?* Do you not see your mistake? Since all things are now ready,

and the Holy Spirit not quite grieved away from your heart by your delay, will you wait any longer?

Does your heart now say, " Lord, I believe: help thou mine unbelief?" Will you take the Saviour *at his word?* Are you willing to trust him to do *the whole work* of your salvation?

If so, prostrate yourself before this waiting, insulted, and still compassionate Redeemer; tell him all your heart, and he will pardon, accept, and save you.

THE ACT OF FAITH.

"BELIEVE ON THE LORD JESUS CHRIST, AND THOU
SHALT BE SAVED."—ACTS 16:31.

I ONCE saw a lad on the roof of a very
high building, where several men were
at work. He was gazing about with ap-
parent unconcern, when suddenly his
foot slipped, and he fell. In falling, he
caught by a rope and hung suspended in
mid-air, where he could get neither up
nor down, and where it was evident he
could sustain himself but a short time.
He perfectly knew his situation, and expected that in a few moments he must
drop upon the rocks below, and be dashed
to pieces.

At this fearful moment, a kind and
powerful man rushed out of the house,
and standing beneath him with extended
arms, called out, "Let go the rope, and I

will receive you. I can do it. Let go
the rope, and I promise you shall escape
unharmed."

The boy hesitated a moment, and then
quit his hold, and dropped easily and
safely into the arms of his deliverer.

Here, thought I, is an illustration of
faith. Here is a simple *act of faith*. The
boy was sensible of his danger. He saw
his deliverer, and heard his voice. He
believed in him, *trusted* to him; and let-
ting go every other dependence and hope,
dropped into his arms.

So must a sinner distinctly apprehend
his guilt, and *his awful exposure* by nature. He must know where he is, and
what he *needs*, before he will apply to
Christ for help. He must see distinctly
that he *is* a sinner—a transgressor of
God's law, and a rebel against his throne.
He must see that he has incurred the
sentence of the law—that it is a *just* sentence, and that he is liable every moment

to sink and perish under it. He must
see that so far as his own efforts are concerned, there is no possibility of escape.
He cannot pay the debt he has contract-
ed, nor can he in any way diminish it a
farthing. He can make no amends, no
expiation for his past sins. The long
catalogue of his transgressions stands
arrayed against him; and for aught he
can do, there it must stand. The sentence of the law has been passed upon
him, and for aught he can do, it must be
speedily executed; and if it is executed,
it will sink him for ever, for this sentence
is no other than eternal death: "eternal
destruction from the presence of the Lord,
and from the glory of his power." 2 Thess.
1 : 9. In this awfully exposed, and so far
as he is concerned, helpless and hopeless
condition, he must see himself before he
will consent to drop into the arms of the
Saviour, and accept deliverance on the
conditions of the gospel.

And he must see more than this. He must see *who the Saviour is*, and *what he has done*, and what is his ability and readiness to save. Suppose the boy suspended by the rope had seen another little boy, like himself, come out of the house and stretch his weak arms, and call upon him to trust to him for deliverance. He would have cried out at once, "You cannot save me. Get out of the way, or I shall fall and crush myself and you." Just so the convicted sinner feels, when invited to put his trust in a man like himself. "A mere human deliverer," he exclaims—"do you mean to mock me? What can such a deliverer do for a wretch like me? What can he do with those mountains of guilt which are pressing upon me, and with that deathless worm which is gnawing within me? What can he do with the dreadful sentence of the law which hangs over me, and with the devouring flames which are kindled to

consume me?" The sinner feels now that
he needs a divine Saviour—an almighty
Saviour—one who is able to "save to the
uttermost"—one whose "blood cleans-
eth from all sin." He feels that no other
Saviour can meet the fearful exigencies
of his case, or can ever do him any good.
And when he looks into the Bible, and
finds that just such a Saviour is provided
and freely offered; when he finds that he
is a holy Saviour, whose word is truth—
a glorious Saviour, altogether deserving
his confidence and love; when with the
eye of faith he sees this Saviour standing
beneath him, and extending his mighty
arms to receive him, and calling out to
him to let go all his false dependences
and hopes, and drop at once into his faithful hands, what should prevent him from
doing it—from simply putting forth *the
act of faith*, and falling into the kind and
gracious arms of his Deliverer? He ob-
viously has all the knowledge and con-

viction that are necessary, and he has only now to believe in Christ, to trust to him, to fall into his embrace, and live for ever.

But suppose a man while hanging, as it were, over the jaws of death, begins to *doubt the ability* or the *readiness* of Christ to save. Suppose he begins to reason with himself, " My soul is of great value, and the difficulties in the way of my salvation are great. How do I know that this Jesus can save me—that he can cleanse such a polluted heart, and rescue such a vile and guilty sinner? Or if he can, how do I know that he will? He may not be sincere in his offers. It may be, he only intends to trifle with my misery." Would not this be a high affront and indignity offered to the benevolent Saviour? Would it not provoke him soon to withdraw his gracious hand, and say, " Well, sinner, if you are determined not to be saved, then you must perish. If you will not *trust in me*, I can do nothing for you. You might have been delivered, if you had hearkened to my voice; but now you must be cast off for ever."

Or suppose that while the Saviour is crying, " Look unto me, and be ye saved," you should say, "*I am not worthy* to come to Christ as I now am. I must wait till I have done something to recommend me to his regards." And suppose the Saviour should continue crying, " Come just as you are; come in all your vileness, and be cleansed in the fountain of my blood;" and you still hold back and persist in the struggle, and hang upon the vain excuse; might he not be expected soon to withdraw, and leave an unbelieving rebel to perish?

Or suppose you should say, "*How came I* to be a sinner? Why did God permit me to sin, or permit sin to come into the world?" Or, " How can I believe of myself? Is not faith the gift of God; and until the gift is bestowed, what can I do but patiently to wait for it?" Or suppose you fly to the other extreme, and say, "I can believe and secure my salvation whenever I please; I need be in no haste about it. I will put off the work till a more convenient season." Or suppose you allege that you are not yet enough convicted—have not had enough feeling, enough distress to render it possible for you to come to Christ. Suppose you speculate and trifle, and think to throw off present obligation in either of these ways; what must be the feelings of the Saviour in regard to you? Here the poor rebel hangs over the pit of destruction, ready to drop at once into the burning lake; and here the Saviour stands in all his fulness, offering to rescue him, and pleading with him to submit and live. What more likely method could he take to seal and secure his own destruction?

Suppose the boy suspended by the rope, instead of dropping into the arms extended to receive him, had insisted on first knowing how he came to fall—"How came my foot to slip, and I to make this fearful plunge? Why did not the men on the roof take better care of me?" Or suppose he had said, "I have no power to let go the rope. My hands are fast clenched upon it, and how can I open them of myself?" Or, "I can let go, and be delivered at any time, and I choose to hang a little longer. Perhaps I have not yet had enough distress." Would he not be evidently beside himself? And yet such is the conduct of the great mass of sinners, and of serious, awakened sinners under the gospel.

Reader, what is your state? Are you yet in your sins? Do you see your dreadful guilt and exposure? And do you anxiously seek and inquire for deliverance? If not, it will be in vain to direct

you. You will not follow any directions,
if given. But if you see yourself to be
all guilty and exposed; if your feelings
prompt you to inquire, with the trem-
bling jailer, "Sirs, what must I do to be
saved?" then it is easy and pleasant to
direct you, to point you to the compassionate Saviour. There he stands with
outstretched arms, waiting to intercept
your fall. Hear him calling. Hear him
inviting. "Come, come, for all things
are now ready." Sinner, yield to him.
Yield at once. Do not doubt his ability
to save you. Do not doubt the sincerity
of his offers. Do not wait to make yourself better. Do not hesitate or speculate
a moment. Remember that the question
before you is one of *right* and *wrong;*
and it is also one of *salvation* or *destruction.* You cannot delay without adding
to your sin, and hazarding the interests
of your immortal soul. *Now, then, is
your time. Now,* while you are reading

and pondering these lines—*now*, while the pressure of obligation is strong upon you, let go at once every other dependence, and fall into the arms of your all-powerful Deliverer.

"Here, Lord, *I give myself away;*
'T is all that I can do."

"Love so amazing, so divine,
Demands *my soul, my life,* MY ALL."

QUESTIONS AND COUNSEL.

BY REV. ASHBEL GREEN, D. D.

FOR THOSE WHO HOPE THAT A WORK OF SAVING
GRACE HAS BEEN WROUGHT UPON THEIR HEARTS.

QUESTIONS. 1. Have you seen yourself to be, by nature and by practice, a
lost and helpless sinner? Have you not
only seen the sinfulness of particular
acts of transgression, but also that your
heart is the seat and fountain of sin—
that in you naturally there is no good
thing? Has a view of this led you to
despair of help from yourself, to see that
you must be altogether indebted to Christ
for salvation, and to the gracious aid of
the Holy Spirit for strength and ability
rightly to perform any duty?

2. On what has your hope of acceptance with God been founded? On your

reformation? on your sorrow for your
sins? on your prayers? on your tears?
on your good works and religious obser-
vances? or has it been on Christ alone,
as your all in all? Has Christ ever ap-
peared very precious to you? Do you
mourn that he does not appear more so?
Have you sometimes felt great freedom
to commit your soul to him? In doing
this, if you have done it, has it been, not
only to be delivered from the punishment
due to your sins, but also from the power, pollution, dominion, and existence of
sin in your soul?

3. As far as you know yourself, do you
hate, and desire to be delivered from all
sin, without any exception of a favorite
lust? Do you pray much to be delivered
from sin? Do you watch against it, and
against temptation to it? Do you strive
against it, and in some degree get the victory over it? Have you so repented of it
as to have your soul really set against it?

4. Have you counted the cost of following Christ, or of being truly religious? That it will cut you off from vain amusement, from the indulgence of your lusts, and from a sinful conformity to the world? That it may expose you to ridicule and contempt, possibly to more serious persecution? In the view of all these things, are you willing to take up the cross, and to follow Christ whithersoever he shall lead you? Is it your solemn purpose, in reliance on his grace and aid, to cleave to him, and to his cause and people to the end of life?

5. Do you love holiness? Do you earnestly desire to be more and more conformed to God and to his holy law; to bear more and more the likeness of your Redeemer? Do you seek, and sometimes find communion with your God and Saviour?

6. Are you resolved, in God's strength, to endeavor conscientiously to perform

your whole duty to God, to your neighbor, and to yourself?

7. Do you make conscience of secret prayer daily? Do you not sometimes feel a backwardness to this duty? Do you at other times feel a great delight in it? Have you a set time and place and order of exercises for performing this duty?

8. Do you daily read a portion of the holy Scriptures in a devout manner? Do you love to read the Bible? Do you ever perceive a sweetness in the truths of holy Scripture? Do you find them adapted to your necessities, and see at times a wonderful beauty, excellence, and glory in God's word? Do you make it the man of your counsel, and endeavor to have both your heart and life conformed to its doctrines and requisitions?

9. Have you ever attempted to covenant with God; to give yourself away to him solemnly and irrevocably, hoping for acceptance through Christ alone; and

taking God in Christ as the covenant God, and satisfying portion of your soul?

10. Does the glory of God ever appear to you as the first, greatest, and best of all objects?

11. Do you feel a love to mankind such as you did not formerly feel? Have you a great desire that the souls of men should be saved, by being brought to a genuine faith and trust in the Redeemer? Do you love God's people with a peculiar attachment because they bear their Saviour's image, and because they love and pursue the objects and delight in the exercises which are most pleasing and delightful to yourself?

12. Do you feel it to be very important to adorn religion by a holy, exemplary, amiable, and blameless walk and conversation? Do you fear to bring a reproach on the cause of Christ? Does this appear to you extremely dreadful? Are you afraid of backsliding, and of being

left to return to a state of carelessness and indifference in religion?

13. Do you desire and endeavor to grow in grace, and in the knowledge of Christ your Saviour more and more? Are you willing to sit at his feet as a little child, and to submit your reason and understanding implicitly to his teaching, imploring his Spirit to guide you into all necessary truth, to save you from fatal errors, to enable you to receive the truth in the love of it, and to transform you more and more into a likeness to himself?

Counsel. 1. Remember that these questions are intended to point your attention to subjects of inquiry the most important. Do not, therefore, content yourself with a careless or cursory reading of them. Read and deliberate, and examine yourself closely on the questions under each head; and let your heart be lifted up to God, while you are considering each particular question, in earnest desire that he may show you the very truth. You cannot ordinarily go over all these questions at one time. Divide them, therefore, and take one part at one time, and another at another. But try to get over the whole in the course of a week; and do this every week for some months. When you find yourself doubtful or deficient in any point, let it not discourage you; but note down that point in writing, and bend the attention of your mind to it, and labor and pray till you shall have made the attainment which will enable you to answer clearly.

2. Remember that secret prayer, reading the word of God, watchfulness, and self-examination are the great means of preserving comfort in religion, and of growing in grace. In proportion as you are exact and faithful in these, such usually will be your inward peace, and the safety of your state. Unite them all to-

gether, and never cease to practise them while you live.

3. Besides the Bible, keep by you and read, at leisure hours, some author of known piety and excellence, as Baxter's Saints' Rest, Doddridge's Works, etc.

4. Do not suppose that any evidence of a gracious state which at present you may think you possess, will release you from the necessity of maintaining a constant vigilance in time to come, nor from repeated examinations and trials of yourself even to the end of life. Many marks and evidences of a gracious state are set down by pious writers. But they must all come to this: to ascertain what is your *prevalent* temper and character; whether, on the whole, you are increasing in sanctification, or not. If you are, you may be comforted; if not, you have cause to be alarmed. It is only he that endureth to the end that shall be saved.

5. I think it of very great importance

to warn you not to imagine that true religion is confined to the closet, or to the church, even though you apprehend that you have great comfort and freedom there. Freedom and comfort there are indeed most desirable, but true religion reaches to every thing. It alters and sweetens the temper. It goes into every duty, relation, station, and situation of life. If you have true religion, you will have a better spirit; you will be better sons, better scholars, better friends, better members of society, and more exemplary in the discharge of every duty, as the sure consequence of this invaluable possession. And if your religion does not produce these effects, although you may talk of inward comforts, and even of raptures, you have great reason to fear that the whole is a delusion, and that the root of the matter is not in you. "Herein is my Father glorified, that ye bear much fruit; so shall ye be my disciples."

6. Be careful to avoid a gloomy, and to cherish a cheerful temper. Be habitually cheerful, but avoid levity. Mirth and laughter are not always sinful; but let your indulgence in them be clearly innocent, not very frequent, and never of long continuance. Be very humble. Be not talkative. Before experienced Christians, be a hearer rather than a talker. Try in every way, however, to promote religion among your relatives and friends. Win them to it by your amiable temper and exemplary deportment. "Flee youthful lusts." Shun every excitement to them. Guard against dissipation—it extinguishes piety. Be not disconcerted by ridicule and reproach. Your Saviour bore much of these for you. Think of this, and be ashamed of nothing so much as of being ashamed of him. Trust in his protection, live to his praise, and you will spend an eternity in his blissful presence.

SELF-DEDICATION TO GOD

FROM DODDRIDGE'S RISE AND PROGRESS

MY DEAR FRIEND—You have felt your lost condition as a sinner against God. You have felt your need of the atoning blood of Christ. You know that blood can be available for you only by your believing in him, trusting in him, dedicating yourself to him, through the promised aids of the Holy Spirit. To this act of dedication you are now urged by conscience, by the word of God, and by the strivings of the Spirit. And it may be of great use to you, not only to form in your heart the purpose of surrendering yourself to God, but expressly to declare it in the divine presence. Such solemnity in the manner of doing it is certainly very reasonable in the nature of things; and surely it is highly expedient for binding to the Lord such a treacherous heart as we know our own to be.

Do it therefore, but do it *deliberately.* Consider what it is that you are to do, and consider how reasonable it is that it should be done cordially and cheerfully; "not by constraint, but willingly," for in this sense, and in every other, "God loveth a cheerful giver." Nothing can be more evident than that we, the product of his power and the price of his Son's blood, should be his, and his for ever. If you see the matter in its just view, it will be the grief of your soul that you have ever alienated yourself from the blessed God and his service: so far will you be from wishing to continue in that state of alienation another year, or another day, you will rejoice to bring back to him his revolted creature; and as you have in times past "yielded your members as instruments of unrighteousness unto sin," you will delight to "yield yourself unto God as alive from the dead."

The surrender will also be as *entire* as it is *cheerful* and *immediate*. All you are, and all you have, and all you can do— your time, your possessions, your influence over others, will be devoted to him, that for the future it may be employed entirely for him and to his glory. You will desire to keep back nothing from him, but will seriously judge that you are then in the truest and noblest sense your own when you are most entirely his. You are also, on this great occasion, to resign all that you have to the disposal of his wise and gracious providence; not only owning his power, but consenting to his undoubted right to do what he pleases with you and all that he has given you.

Once more, let me remind you that this surrender must be *perpetual*. You must give yourself up to God in such a manner as never more to pretend to be your own; for the rights of God are, like his nature, eternal and immutable; and with regard to his rational creatures, are the same yesterday, to-day, and for ever.

I would further advise and urge, that this dedication may be made with all possible *solemnity*. Do it in express words. And perhaps it may be in many cases most expedient, as many pious divines have recommended, to do it in writing. Set your hand and seal to it, "that on such a day of such a month and year, and at such a place, on full consideration and serious reflection, you came to this happy resolution, that whatsoever others might do, you would serve the Lord."

Such an instrument you may, if you please, draw up for yourself; or, if you rather choose to have it drawn up to your hand, you may find something of this nature below, in which you may easily make such alterations as your cir-

cumstances may seem to require. But
whatever form you use, weigh it well;
meditate attentively upon it, that you
may "not be rash with your mouth to
utter any thing before God." And when
you determine to execute this instrument,
let the transaction be attended with some
more than ordinary religious retirement.
Make it, if you conveniently can, a day
of secret fasting and prayer; and when
your heart is prepared with a becoming
awe of the divine Majesty, with an humble confidence in his goodness, and an
earnest desire of his favor, then present
yourself on your knees before God, and
read it over deliberately and solemnly;
and when you have signed it, lay it by
in some secure place, where you may
review it whenever you please; and
make it a rule with yourself 'to review
it, if possible, at certain seasons of the
year, that you may keep up the remembrance of it. And God grant that you

may be enabled to keep it, and in the whole of your life walk according to it. May it be an anchor to your soul in every temptation, a cordial in every affliction; and may the recollection of it give strength to your departing spirit, in a consciousness that it is ascending to your covenant God and Father, and to that gracious Redeemer whose power and faithfulness will securely "keep what you commit to him unto that day."

AN EXAMPLE OF SELF-DEDICATION.

"Eternal and ever-blessed God, I desire to present myself before thee with the deepest humiliation and abasement of soul, sensible how unworthy such a sinful worm is to appear before the holy Majesty of heaven, the King of kings and Lord of lords, and especially on such an occasion as this, even to dedicate myself, without reserve, to thee. But the scheme and plan is thine own. Thine infinite condescension hath offered it by thy Son, and thy grace hath inclined my heart to accept of it.

"I come, therefore, acknowledging myself to have been a great offender, smiting upon my breast, and saying, with the humble publican, 'God be merciful to me a sinner.' I come, invited by the name of thy Son, and wholly trusting in his perfect righteousness, entreating that for his sake thou wilt be merciful to my unrighteousness, and wilt no more remember my sins. Receive, I beseech thee, thy revolted creature, who is now convinced of thy right to him, and desires nothing so much as that he may be thine.

"This day do I, with the utmost solemnity, surrender myself to thee. I renounce all former lords that have had dominion over me; and I consecrate to thee all that I am, and all that I have; the faculties of my mind, the members of my body, my worldly possessions, my time, and my influence over others, to be

all used entirely for thy glory, and stead-
fastly employed in obedience to thy com-
mands, as long as thou continuest me in
life, with an ardent desire and humble
resolution to continue thine through all
the endless ages of eternity; ever hold-.
ing myself in an attentive posture to observe the first intimations of thy will, and
ready to spring forward with zeal and joy
to the immediate execution of it.

" To thy direction also I resign myself,
and all I am and have, to be disposed of
by thee in such a manner as thou shalt
in thine infinite wisdom judge most sub-
servient to the purposes of thy glory. To
thee I leave the management of all events,
and say without reserve, ' Not my will,
but thine be done;' rejoicing with a loyal
heart in thine unlimited government, as
what ought to be the delight of the whole
rational creation.

" Use me, O Lord, I beseech thee, as an
instrument of thy service. Number me

among thy peculiar people. Let me be washed in the blood of thy dear Son. Let me be clothed with his righteousness. Let me be sanctified by his Spirit. Transform me more and more into his image. Impart to me, through him, all needful influences of thy purifying, cheering, and comforting Spirit. And let my life be spent under those influences, and in the light of thy gracious countenance, as my Father and my God.

"And when the solemn hour of death comes, may I remember thy COVENANT, 'well-ordered in all things and sure, as all my salvation, and all my desire,' 2 Sam. 23 : 5, though every hope and enjoyment is perishing; and do thou, O Lord, remember it too. Look down with pity, O my heavenly Father, on thy languishing, dying child. Embrace me in thine everlasting arms. Put strength and confidence into my departing spirit, and receive it to the abodes of them that sleep in Jesus, peacefully and joyfully to wait the accomplishment of thy great promise to all thy people, even that of a glorious resurrection, and of eternal happiness in thy heavenly presence.

"And if any surviving friend should, when I am in the dust, meet with this memorial of my solemn transactions with thee, may he make the engagement his own; and do thou graciously admit him to partake in all the blessings of THY COVENANT, through Jesus the great Mediator of it; to whom, with thee, O Father, and thy Holy Spirit, be everlasting praises. Amen."

ADVICE TO YOUNG CONVERTS.

BY REV. JONATHAN EDWARDS.

ORIGINALLY ADDRESSED TO A YOUNG LADY AT S——,
CONN., IN THE YEAR 1741.

DEAR YOUNG FRIEND—As you desired
me to send you, in writing, some directions how to conduct yourself in your
Christian course, I would now answer
your request.   The sweet remembrance
of the great things I have lately seen at
S——, inclines me to do any thing in my
power to contribute to the spiritual joy
and prosperity of God's people there.

1. I would advise you to keep up as
great a strife and earnestness in religion,
as if you knew yourself to be in a state
of nature, and were seeking conversion.
We advise persons under conviction to
be earnest and violent for the kingdom
of heaven; but when they have attained

to conversion, they ought not to be the less watchful, laborious, and earnest in the whole work of religion, but the more so, for they are under infinitely greater obligations. For want of this, many persons, in a few months after their conversion, have begun to lose their sweet and lively sense of spiritual things, and to grow cold and dark, and have "pierced themselves through with many sorrows;" whereas, if they had done as the apostle did, Phil. 3 : 12–14, their path would have been "as the shining light, that shines more and more unto the perfect day."

2. Do not leave off seeking, striving, and praying for the very same things that we exhort unconverted persons to strive for, and a degree of which you have had already in conversion. Pray that your eyes may be opened, that you may receive sight, that you may know yourself and be brought to God's footstool, and that you may see the glory of God and

Christ, and may be raised from the dead, and have the love of Christ shed abroad in your heart. Those who have most of these things have need still to pray for them; for there is so much blindness and hardness, pride and death remaining, that they still need to have that work of God wrought upon them, further to enlighten and enliven them, that shall be bringing them out of darkness into God's marvellous light, and be a kind of new conversion and resurrection from the dead. There are very few requests that are proper for an impenitent man, that are not also, in some sense, proper for the godly.

3. When you hear a sermon, hear for yourself. Though what is spoken may be more especially directed to the unconverted, or to those that, in other respects, are in different circumstances from yourself, yet let the chief intent of your mind be to consider, "In what respect is this applicable to me, and what improvement

ought I to make of this for my own soul's good?"

4. Though God has forgiven and forgotten your past sins, yet do not forget them yourself: often remember what a wretched bond-slave you were in the land of Egypt. Often bring to mind your particular acts of sin before conversion, as the blessed apostle Paul is often mentioning his old blaspheming, persecuting spirit, and his injuriousness to the renewed; humbling his heart, and acknowledging that he was "the least of the apostles," and not worthy "to be called an apostle," and the "least of all saints," and the "chief of sinners;" and be often confessing your old sins to God; and let that text be often in your mind, Ezek. 16 : 63, "That thou mayest remember and be confounded, and never open thy mouth any more because of thy shame, when I am pacified towards thee for all that thou hast done, saith the Lord God."

5. Remember that you have more cause, on some accounts, a thousand times, to lament and humble yourself for sins that have been committed since conversion than before—because of the infinitely greater obligations that are upon you to live to God—and to look upon the faithfulness of Christ in unchangeably continuing his loving-kindness, notwithstanding all your great unworthiness since your conversion.

6. Be always greatly abashed for your remaining sin, and never think that you lie low enough for it; but yet be not discouraged or disheartened by it; for though we are exceeding sinful, yet we have an advocate with the Father, Jesus Christ the righteous, the preciousness of whose blood, the merit of whose righteousness, and the greatness of whose love and faithfulness infinitely overtop the highest mountains of our sins.

7. When you engage in the duty of

prayer, or come to the Lord's supper, or attend any other duty of divine worship, come to Christ as Mary Magdalen did, Luke 7:37, 38; come and cast yourself at his feet, and kiss and pour forth upon him the sweet perfumed ointment of divine love, out of a pure and broken heart, as she poured the precious ointment out of her pure broken alabaster box.

8. Remember, that pride is the worst viper that is in the heart, the greatest disturber of the soul's peace and of sweet communion with Christ: it was the first sin committed, and lies lowest in the foundation of Satan's whole building, and is with the greatest difficulty rooted out, and is the most hidden, secret, and deceitful of all lusts, and often creeps insensibly into the midst of religion, even sometimes under the disguise of humility itself.

9. That you may pass a correct judgment concerning yourself, always look

upon those as the best discoveries and the best comforts that have most of these two effects: those that make you least and lowest, and most like a child, and those that most engage and fix your heart in a full and firm disposition to deny youself for God, and to spend and be spent for him.

10. If at any time you fall into doubts about the state of your soul, in dark and dull frames of mind, it is proper to review your past experience; but do not consume too much time and strength in this way: rather apply yourself, with all your might, to an earnest pursuit after renewed experience, new light, and new lively acts of faith and love. One new discovery of the glory of Christ's face will do more towards scattering clouds of darkness in one minute, than examining old experiences by the best marks that can be given, through a whole year.

11. When the exercise of grace is low,

and corruption prevails, and by that
means fear prevails, do not desire to have
fear cast out any other way than by the
reviving and prevailing of love in the
heart; by this, fear will be effectually
expelled, as darkness in a room vanishes
away when the pleasant beams of the
sun are let into it.

12. When you counsel and warn others, do it earnestly and affectionately and
thoroughly; and when you are speaking
to your equals, let your warnings be in-
termixed with expressions of your sense
of your own unworthiness, and of the
sovereign grace that makes you differ.

13. If you would set up religious meetings of young women by yourselves, to
be attended once in a while besides the
other meetings that you attend, I should
think it would be very proper and profit-
able.

14. Under special difficulties, or when
in great need of, or great longings after

any particular mercy for yourself or others, set apart a day for secret prayer and fasting by yourself alone; and let the day be spent not only in petitions for the mercies you desire, but in searching your heart, and in looking over your past life, and confessing your sins before God, not as is wont to be done in public prayer, but by a very particular rehearsal before God of the sins of your past life, from your childhood hitherto, before and after conversion, with the circumstances and aggravations attending them, spreading all the abominations of your heart very particularly and fully as possible before God.

15. Do not let the adversaries of the cross have occasion to reproach religion on your account. How holily should the children of God, the redeemed and the beloved of the Son of God, behave themselves. Therefore, "walk as children of the light and of the day," and

"adorn the doctrine of God your Saviour;" and especially abound in what are called the Christian virtues, and make you like the Lamb of God; be meek and lowly of heart, and full of pure, heavenly, and humble love to all; abound in deeds of love to others, and self-denial for others; and let there be in you a disposition to account others better than yourself.

16. In all your course, walk with God and follow Christ as a little, poor, helpless child, taking hold of Christ's hand, keeping your eye on the marks of the wounds in his hand and side, whence came the blood that cleanses you from sin, and hiding your nakedness under the skirt of the white shining robes of his righteousness.

17. Pray much for the ministers and the church of God, especially that he would carry on his glorious work which he has now begun, till the world shall be full of his glory.

THE CLOSET COMPANION,

OR

A HELP TO SELF-EXAMINATION.

DIRECTIONS.

I. *Make conscience of performing this duty.* The necessity of it will appear if you consider, 1. God has repeatedly commanded it. 2. The people of God have always practised it. 3. There is great danger of being deceived, for every grace in the Christian has its counterfeit in the hypocrite. 4. Many professors have been deceived by neglecting it, and are ruined for ever. 5. Your comfort depends, in a great measure, upon knowing your real state.

II. *Be very serious in the performance of it.* Set your heart to the solemn work as in the presence of the Searcher of hearts, who will judge the secrets of all men in the great day. Heaven and hell are no trifles. The question before you is no less than this: Am I a child of wrath, or a child of God? If I should die when I have done reading this, where would this precious soul of mine be for ever?

III. *Be impartial,* or you lose your labor; nay, you confirm your mistakes. On the other hand, resolve to know the *worst* of yourself, the very worst. Some are afraid to know the worst, lest they should fall into despair; and this fear makes them partial. Suppose the worst, and if, after serious examination, it should appear that you have neither faith nor repentance, yet remember your case is not desperate. The door of mercy is ever open to the returning sinner. It remains a blessed truth, that *whosoever cometh to Christ shall in no wise be cast out.*

On the other hand, be willing to know the *best* of yourself, as well as the *worst.* Do not suppose that humility requires you to overlook your graces, and notice only your corruptions.

IV. Judge of your graces by their *nature* rather than their *degree.* You are to try inherent graces by the *touchstone*, not by the *measure.* The greatest degree is to be desired and aimed at, but the smallest degree is matter of praise and rejoicing. Do not conclude there is no grace because there is some corruption, or that the Spirit does not strive against the flesh because the flesh strives against the Spirit.

V. Let not the issue of this trial depend at all upon the knowledge of the *exact time* of your conversion, or the particular minister or sermon first instrumental in it. Many are wrought upon by slow and insensible degrees. Grace increases like the daylight. No man doubts whether the sun shines at noon because he did not see the day break.

VI. Take this caution, lest you stumble at the threshold. The question before you is not, Will God accept and save me, though a vile sinner, if I believe on Christ? But you are to inquire, *Am I now, at this time, in an accepted state?* The former question is already resolved by God himself, who cannot lie. His word positively declares that every returning sinner shall be accepted and saved. This being determined, is not to be questioned. But you are to try whether you are *now* in a state of grace.

VII. Take care that you do not trust in your *self-examination* rather than in *Christ.* There is a proneness in our natures to put duties in the place of Christ.

VIII. Be not content merely to *read* over the following questions, but stop and dwell on each; nor suffer yourself to proceed to another till you have put the first home to your conscience, and have got an honest answer to it.

IX. Examine yourself *frequently*. Seek every opportunity to do it. The Lord's-day evening is a most suitable season. The oftener you perform this work, the easier it will become. If you do not obtain satisfaction at first, you may by repeated endeavors; and a scriptural, solid hope will amply repay your utmost labor.

RESPECTING FAITH AND ITS FRUITS.

I. DO I BELIEVE ON THE SON OF GOD? Surely this is an important question. My Bible assures me, that "he that believeth shall be saved." Do I then believe? And here let me carefully distinguish between faith and its fruits. What is faith? The simple meaning of faith is believing; and believing always refers to something spoken or written. Divine faith is the belief of a divine testimony, as John speaks, "He that hath received his testimony, hath set to his seal that *God is true.*" And on the contrary, the apostle John says, "He that believeth not God, hath made him a liar, because he believeth not the record that God gave of his Son. And this is the record that God hath given to us eternal life, and this life is in his Son." I must first believe the *truth* of God, as revealed in his word; I must credit his report, and believe his testimony concerning Christ; and then *receive* and *trust in Christ* so revealed for my own personal salvation. But to be more particular,

1. Do I really believe that I am a fallen creature; that I derived from Adam a nature wholly corrupt, depraved, and sinful; and that I am a child of wrath by nature even as others? Have I ever considered the unspotted and infinite purity and holiness of God's nature, and that he abhors sin wherever he sees it? Have I considered that his law, contained in

the ten commandments, is a copy and transcript of that holy nature; and by comparing myself with that eternal rule of right, have I been led to see my horrible wickedness and vileness? O what multitudes of sins have I committed in thought, word, and deed. Am I really sick of sin, sorry for sin, and do I abhor myself as a vile sinner?

2. Have I duly considered what my sins have deserved? Do I sincerely think that if God had sent me to hell because of my sins, he would have done justly?

3. Do I see my utter helplessness, as well as my sin and misery? Am I perfectly assured that I cannot by any works, duties, or sufferings of my own, save myself; but that if ever I am saved, it must be the effect of free mercy?

4. Are the eyes of my understanding enlightened to know Christ? What do I think of Christ? Who is he? Do I believe that he is *God manifest in the*

flesh, uniting in his *one* person the human and divine natures: *man* that he might suffer, and *God* that he might redeem? Do I know *why* he suffered; that it was to make satisfaction to divine justice for the injury done to God's law and government by man's sin? Do I believe that the Father "is well pleased for his righteousness' sake, and that he has magnified the law and made it honorable?" Do I therefore look upon Christ as the only way to the Father—as the only foundation to build on, the only fountain to wash in? Am I persuaded of his ability "to save to the uttermost all who come to God by him?"

5. Am I satisfied from God's own word and promise, that whoever, let him be ever so vile and wicked, cometh to Christ by faith, shall be saved—the promise being without exception, "Whosoever believeth on him shall not be ashamed?"

6. Am I led and assisted by the Spirit of God to believe this general promise in *my own particular case?* As God has made no exceptions, why should I except myself? True, no tongue can tell how vile I have been; only God knows the greatness of my sins and the wickedness of my heart. But shall I then *reject Christ, and despair,* and so add to my other sins the worst and greatest sin of all, *unbelief?* God forbid. "It is a faithful saying, and worthy of all acceptation, that Christ came to save sinners." Do I then, sensible of my sin, misery, and helplessness, look upon Christ as an all-sufficient Saviour, and commit my precious and immortal soul to him, relying upon him only, and endeavoring to rely upon him confidently for eternal salvation?

Having thus examined my faith, let me proceed impartially to examine the *fruits and effects of my faith.* Many pretend to faith whose works give the lie to their pretensions; let me therefore "show my faith by my works."

II. WHAT ARE THE FRUITS OF MY FAITH? Does it produce those effects which the word of God points out as the proof and evidence of its sincerity, with respect to my *conscience,* my *heart,* and my *life?*

1. What are the effects of my faith as to my *conscience?* Do I rest from my former legal attempt to justify myself, going about to establish my own righteousness? Am I satisfied with Christ's righteousness as a complete title to glory? I read of "peace in believing;" have I peace in my conscience? Being justified by faith, have I peace with God? When my soul is alarmed by the remembrance of former sins, or those lately committed, how do I obtain peace? Is it by forgetting them as soon as I can, and then fancying that God has forgotten them too? Is it by resolving to do so no more, and so mak-

ing future obedience atone for past offences? Is it by performing religious duties, and so making amends? Or is it by a fresh application to the pardoning, peace-speaking blood of Christ? When my sins stare me in the face, and my duties themselves appear sins, whence, O my soul, proceeds thy comfort? Is it the blood of Christ that "purges my conscience from dead works?" Does faith in the atonement free me from the dreadful apprehension of condemnation and wrath due to sin? Do I, or do I not look up to God, through the death of his Son, with freedom and delight? If I have not this peace, why is it? What hinders? Either I do not clearly understand the nature of the gospel, or I do not fully believe it; for it provides for every possible case. If I have this, blessed be God for it. Lord, help me to keep it, that it may keep me. Lord, I believe; help thou my unbelief

2. What are the effects of my faith as to my *heart and its affections?*

(1.) *Do I love God the Father?* Do I think of him, and go to him as a loving Father in Christ? Have I the spirit of adoption, so that I cry, *Abba, Father?* Do I love him as the Father of mercies, the God of hope, the God of peace, the God of love?

(2.) *Do I love Christ?* To those who believe, he is precious; is he precious to me? Do I see infinite beauty in his person? Is he the chief among ten thousands to me, and altogether lovely? Do I admire the length and breadth and depth and height of his love? Is the language of my very soul, *None but Christ, none but Christ?* Is it my grief and shame that I love him no more?

(3.) *Do I love the Holy Spirit?* Do I honor him as the great Author of light and life, grace and comfort? Do I maintain a deep sense of my dependence on

his agency in all my religious perform-
ances? Do I desire my heart to be his
temple? Am I cautious lest I quench his
holy motions, or grieve him by my sins?
Am I sensible that without his influence
I cannot pray, hear, read, communicate,
nor examine myself as I ought?

(4.) *Do I love God's law?* Do I delight
in the law of the Lord after the inward
man, not wishing it less strict and holy,
but loving it because it is holy? Am I
as willing to take Christ for my *King* to
rule over me, as for my *Priest* to atone
for me? Do I hunger and thirst after
righteousness? Do I pant and long and
pray to be holy? Do I wish to be holy,
as I wish to be happy? Do I hate all
sin, especially that sin which most easily
besets me, and labor daily to mortify it
and to deny myself? Do I sigh for complete deliverance from remaining corruption, and rejoice in the hope of it, through
a holy Jesus? Do I long for heaven, that

there I may be satisfied with his likeness?

(5.) *Do I love God's people?* Can I say to Christ, as Ruth to Naomi, "Thy people shall be my people?" Do I love them because they love Christ and bear his image? Do I feel a union of spirit with them, though they may not be of my party, or think exactly as I do? Can I say, "I know that I have passed from death to life, because I love the brethren?"

3. What are the effects of my faith as to my *daily walk and conversation?* The word of God tells me that he who is in Christ is a "new creature; old things are passed away; all things are become new." "If ye love me," said Christ, "keep my commandments." Let me review the commandments, and see how my love to Christ is manifested by my obedience.

(1.) Do I know and acknowledge God to be the only true God, and my God, and

do I worship and glorify him accordingly?
Is he the supreme object of my desire and
delight? Do I trust him, hope in him,
love to think of him? Do I pray to him; do
I praise him; am I careful to please him?

(2.) Do I receive, observe, and keep
pure and entire all such religious worship
and ordinances as God hath appointed in
his word? How is it with me in secret
prayer, in family prayer, in public prayer? With what views do I go to hear
the preached gospel, and what good do I
get by it?

(3.) Do I make a holy and reverent use
of God's names, titles, attributes, ordinances, word, and works, avoiding the
profanation or abuse of any thing where-
by God makes himself known?

(4.) Do I keep holy to God the Sabbath-
day, resting all that day from worldly
employments, recreations, and conversation? And do I spend the *whole time* in
public and private exercises of divine

worship, except so much as is to be taken up in the works of necessity and mercy? Is the Sabbath my delight, and are the ordinances of God's house very precious to my soul?

(5.) Do I endeavor to preserve the honor and perform all the duties which I owe to my superiors, inferiors, or equals—remembering that true religion makes good husbands, wives, children, masters, and servants? If I am *really* holy, I am *relatively* holy.

(6.) Do I use all lawful means to preserve my own life and the life of others? Do I avoid all intemperance? Do I resist passionate tempers? Do I labor to promote the welfare of men's souls? Do I exercise love and compassion towards the poor and distressed according to my ability? Do I freely forgive those who have injured me? Do I pray for them; and instead of hating, do I love my very enemies?

(7.) Do I earnestly strive to preserve my own and my neighbor's *chastity* in heart, speech, and behavior, avoiding all incentives to lust, such as intemperance in food, lascivious songs, books, pictures, dancing, plays, and vile company, remembering that my body is the temple of the Holy Ghost?

(8.) Do I use the lawful means of procuring and furthering the wealth and outward estate of myself and others? Do I abhor every species of robbery and injustice? Am I strictly and conscientiously honest in all my dealings, not overreaching nor defrauding any person in any degree?

(9.) Do I studiously maintain and promote truth between man and man, not only abhorring perjury, but hating all falsehood? And do I, as a professor of religion, avoid both ludicrous and pernicious lies, being as tender of my neighbor's character as of my own? Am I very cautious in making promises, and very careful to keep them?

(10.) Am I contented with the condition God has allotted me, believing that he orders all things for the best? And do I avoid envying my neighbor's happiness, or inordinately desiring any thing that is his?

CONCLUSION. And now, dear reader, what is the result of your inquiry? Have you made a solemn pause at the close of every question, and obtained an honest answer? And are you, notwithstanding many imperfections, able to conclude that your faith is of God's operation, and proved so to be by its holy fruits? Then take the comfort, and give God the glory.

But if, on the other hand, the evidence of Scripture and your conscience is against you, and you are forced to conclude that your heart is not right with God, then for God's sake, and for your soul's sake, cry instantly and mightily to him to have mercy upon you; remembering, that though your case is awful, it is not desperate; and that still you, even you, coming to Christ, shall in no wise be cast out.

SIGNS OF A LIVING

OR

GROWING CHRISTIAN.

"THE RIGHTEOUS SHALL FLOURISH LIKE THE PALM-TREE; HE SHALL GROW LIKE A CEDAR IN LEBA-NON." Psa. 92:12.

1. When your chief delight is with the saints, especially them that excel in virtue. Psa. 16:3.

2. When the smitings of the righteous are not a burden to you, and you can hear of your faults with affectionate attention. Psa. 141:5.

3. When reproach for Christ makes you not ashamed of Christ. Mark 8:38; Heb. 11:26.

4. When wandering thoughts, in time of duty, find less entertainment than formerly. Psa. 139:23; 1 Cor. 13:11.

5 When length of standing in the profession of Christianity, works increase of hatred to all sin. Psa. 119 : 104–113.

6. When you carry about with you a constant jealousy over your own heart, that it turn not aside from God and goodness. Prov. 18 : 14.

7. When every known mercy begets new thankfulness, and that with delight. Psa. 145 : 2.

8. When known calamity in God's house begets deep sorrow in your heart. Neh. 1 : 4.

9. When, under deep distress or languishing, the word of God is precious to you. Psa. 119 : 92.

10. When any condition in the world, though in itself mean, as it comes from God is most welcome. Job 1 : 21; Hab 3 : 17, 18.

11. When your chief care, to avoid all sin, is as truly occasioned through fear of dishonoring God and incurring his pres-

ent displeasure, as of *the wrath to come*. Neh. 5 : 15 ; Gen. 39 : 9.

12. When every company is burdensome to you, that is not designing your Father's glory, but derogating therefrom. Psa. 120 : 5 ; 2 Peter, 2 : 7, 8.

13. When the sins of others come so near your heart that you walk sadly to see such persons transgress God's commandments. Psa. 119 : 136.

14. When the company of the pious poor is preferred to that of the ungodly rich.

15. When it is truly painful to you to see sinners going heedlessly on in the broad road to ruin.

16. When you are willing to part with all for Christ.

17. When the yoke of self-denial, as imposed by Christ Jesus, is not grievous, but pleasant to you. Matt. 11 : 29, 30 ; Mark 10 : 28.

18. When increase of time in Christ's

acquaintance, works increase of delight in communion with Christ. Psalm 92 : 12–14.

19. When the majesty of the great God, considering how visible you are in his sight, has an awful prevalence upon your heart. Job 31 : 4.

20. When you are at open war and constant hostility with *bosom sin*, as displeasing to God, and forbidden by his law. Psa. 18 : 23.

21. When you have a thirsting desire to get the power of godliness in your heart, rather than the form of godliness in the head, or outward profession. 2 Cor. 1 : 12.

22. When the worship of God, agreeable to his word, is highly prized and faithfully practised in the worst of times. Mal. 3 : 14–16.

23. When the soul is more hungry for the word of God, than the body is for temporal food. Job 23 : 12; Psa. 119 : 72, 162.

SIGNS OF A DYING

OR

DECAYING CHRISTIAN.

1. WHEN you are so indifferent to public worship, or frequenting the church of God, that you can be satisfied to come, or not come, at your own pleasure.

2. When, in your most solemn worship, you are quickly weary without warrantable cause.

3. When few sermons will please you; either you like not the *matter*, or *manner*, or *man*, or *place*.

4. When you think you know enough.

5. When a small occasion will keep you from Christ's table, or communion with the church of God.

6. When you have usually no great desire for prayer.

7. When reading the holy Scriptures is more burdensome than delightful.

8. When you are very inquisitive after novelties or new things, rather than wholesome doctrine.

9. When you are so little prepared for the solemn assemblies, that they come before you think of them, or long for them.

10. When you come to the assembly more for fear of the brethren's eye, than Christ's omniscient and all-piercing eye.

11. When you will rather betray the name of Christ Jesus and the credit of his gospel by your silence, than appear for it to your own suffering and disparagement.

12. When, at a small offence, you are usually so impatient that you commit great sin.

13. When you are more careful to get the words of Christ's people than the spirit of Christ's people, the *form* than the *power*.

14. When you are not much troubled

at your own miscarriages, while they are kept from *public view.*

15 When you love *least* those Christians that deal most faithfully with you, in showing you your faults and pointing you to the remedy.

16. When you pray more that afflictions may be removed than sanctified.

17. When under God's calamity you find neither the need nor the benefit of humbling yourself by fasting and prayer.

18. When the thought of your bosom-lust, or any other sin, is more prevalent with you than pleasing God.

19. When you are curious about the lesser matters of God's law, and careless about the weightier.

20. When the Holy Spirit's help to the great work of mortification seems not of absolute necessity to you.

21. When you are so ignorant of your spiritual standing that you know not whether you grow or decay.

22. When great sins seem smaller, and small sins seem none at all.

23. When a watchful care of a godly life and a Christian conversation is more accidental than habitual.

24. When care for your body is usually most pleasant, and care for your soul usually most irksome.

25. When you are much a stranger to the practical part of meditation on the word and works of God.

26. When the thoughts of a dying Jesus for your sins little dissuade you from an unchristian conversation.

27. When you can commit sin without pain, and reflect upon it with indifference.

28. When you find greater satisfaction in the company of the world than with the people of God.

DIRECTIONS.

I. TO ASSIST IN ATTAINING A SPIRIT OF PRAYER.

1. Renounce all known sin and sensual indulgence.

2. Be not conformed to the world.

3. Resist the temptations of Satan.

4. Beware of a self-righteous spirit.

5. Look for aid of the Holy Spirit.

6. Trust only in the name of Christ.

7. Be watchful. Watch for favorable opportunities of prayer. Watch over your heart in prayer. Watch for answers to your prayers. Meditate before you pray. Meditate on the promises and presence of God. Ask his gracious help, and the teaching of his Spirit. Lay aside all malice, guile, envy, hatred. Remember thy own vileness, and God's awful majesty. Be humble. Disburden thy mind of worldly thoughts and cares.

8 Ask in faith.

9. Aim to enjoy a holy freedom and boldness of access to God.

10. Be sincere and fervent.

11. Be frequent and persevering.

12. Be humble and self-abased.

II. TO THOSE WHO WOULD GROW IN GRACE.

1. *Search the Scriptures.* Let no book supplant the Bible. Love its truths, and study to know *all* that it reveals.

2. *Pray without ceasing.* Neglect of the closet will bring leanness into your soul. Have stated seasons of prayer, with which no worldly interest must be allowed to interfere.

3. *Guard against a worldly spirit.* Love not the world. Set your affections on heavenly things. "No man can serve two masters."

4. *Love the brethren.* Be not too careful to note their faults and imperfections. "Let each esteem other better than him-

self." " Speak not evil one of another."
" Behold how pleasant it is for brethren
to dwell together in unity."

5. *Watch narrowly your own heart.* Be
constantly jealous of it, lest it turn aside
from God.

6. *Cultivate a liberal and benevolent
spirit.* Remember you are not your own.
When Christ calls for your substance,
freely give it. Sustain properly the institutions of the gospel. Contribute for
the cause of missions, the Tract, the Bible, and all the great objects of Christian
benevolence. Nothing so much dwarfs
the spiritual growth of the Christian as
a want of liberality. Christ loves a
cheerful giver.

7. Punctually attend on the ordinances of the church. Be present both at
the services of the Sabbath, and through
the week. The church suffers deeply
from the laxity of her members in sus-
taining her institutions.

8. Be active in extending the cause of Christ. Do this by fervent prayer, by a holy and blameless life, and by judicious efforts to convert sinners.

9. Finally, when you have done all, esteem yourself an unprofitable servant, and ascribe all the glory to God and the Lamb.

III. FOR PROFITABLY READING THE SCRIPTURES.

1. With earnest prayer for the teaching of the Spirit, and in entire dependence upon its truth. Read the Bible in the spirit of continual prayer—prayer before you begin, prayer mixed with your reading, and prayer when you have done.

2. Mix faith with all you read.

3. Read the Bible with great reverence, and with an humble and teachable mind.

3. Read with patient meditation, self-application, and self-examination.

5. Read with simplicity of mind, de-

siring to be instructed in the truth of God, and with a single eye to the salvation of your soul.

6. Read with a heart devoted to God.

7. Read habitually, regularly, and at *stated* periods.

8. Compare one part of the Scripture with another.

ON

THE KNOWLEDGE OF PARDON

AND

THE WITNESS OF THE SPIRIT.

THOUGH, in some cases, persons may know the time and the place, both when they were awakened and when they were comforted; yea, when they were brought to submit to God's righteousness in their condemnation, notwithstanding all their endeavors, and to cast themselves on his free mercy through the blood of Jesus, and to see his whole character and conduct lovely, and Christ precious, and his salvation glorious, and holiness beautiful, and his service perfect freedom; yet it is not generally thus. At first, knowledge is usually scanty, experiences are indistinct, and views of divine things are confused and mixed with inconsistency. Then shall ye know, if ye follow on to

know the Lord: his going forth is prepared as the morning. Now, in the
morning the day dawns; a glimmering
beam diffuses itself, but it is dusk still,
and objects are indistinctly perceived: but
gradually it grows lighter. Thus it com-
monly is with true Christians. In time,
they find that these effects are produced;
and if they are certainly produced, it
matters not whether we know when or
where. If God hath shown you the
strictness and goodness of the law, and
your obligations as the creature to love
and obey him according to it, so as to
convince you that by nature and practice you are an inexcusable sinner, deserving of his wrath; that none of your
doings can make him your debtor, or give
you any claim upon his justice, or make
it unjust in him to condemn you: if you
see your best deeds to be sinful, and to need
forgiveness; and seeing this, take the
blame to yourself, cast yourself on free

mercy as a justly condemned sinner—see a suitableness in God's way of saving sinners, through the infinitely valuable obedience and atonement of Emmanuel, honoring the law, and satisfying justice in our stead, that he *might be just and the justifier* of the ungodly: if you have thus learnt to see God's whole character love-ly—that one so great and glorious, so holy and just, should be so compassion-ate, merciful, and loving; if in this way you have learned to hate sin, to love ho-liness and follow after it, and to be hum-bled, ashamed, and grieved that you are no more holy—to feel a spirit of cordial love to God's character, government, and gospel, gratitude to him for his mercies, zeal for his glory—wanting others to know, love, serve, and enjoy his favor—considering his cause as yours, being grieved when his name is dishonored, and rejoicing in the prosperity of religion—praying from your heart the beginning of the Lord's prayer; if this has taught you to desire to be patient in trouble, to be contented in your station, to depend on his providence, to adorn his gospel, and live to his glory, you then have the substantial evidences of conversion, such as they who have the most of the others have in general little of.   This filial spirit towards God is *the spirit of adoption—the seal of the Spirit*, which the devil can neither break nor counterfeit—*the earnest of the Spirit*, a part of heaven brought down into the soul as a pledge of the whole.   And when the Holy Ghost brings these implanted graces into lively, vigorous exercise, then he *witnesses with our spirits that we are God's children*, and not usually by any words brought to the mind, as many are deluded to believe.   The latter, Satan can counterfeit, and it has nothing divine in it; the former is divine, from God, and leading to God.

DR. SCOTT.

SCRIPTURE COUNSELS.

BEHOLD what manner of love the Father hath bestowed upon us, that we should be called the *sons of God*. God, who is rich in mercy, for his great love wherewith he loved us, even when we were dead in sins, hath quickened us together with Christ, and hath raised us up together, and made us sit together in heavenly places in Christ Jesus. For ye *were* as sheep going astray, but are now returned unto the Shepherd and Bishop of your souls.

Be ye followers of God as dear children, and walk worthy of the vocation wherewith ye are called. For ye were sometime darkness, but now are ye light in the Lord; walk as children of the light. If ye then be risen with Christ, seek those things which are above, where Christ sitteth on the right hand of God. Set your affection on things above, not on things on the earth. The world passeth away, and the lust thereof; but he that doeth the will of God abideth for ever. For *this is the love of God*, that we *keep his commandments*. And we have known and believed the love which God hath towards us. God is love; and he that dwelleth in love dwelleth in God, and God in him. Know ye not that your bodies are the temple of the Holy Ghost? And ye are not your own, for ye are bought with a price; therefore glorify God in your bodies and in your spirits, which are his.

Search the Scriptures, for in them ye think ye have eternal life. The commandments of the Lord are pure, enlightening the eyes: more to be desired are they than gold, yea, than much fine gold; sweeter also than honey and the honeycomb. Let the word of God *dwell* in you *richly*, teaching and admonishing one

another in psalms and hymns and spiritual songs, singing with grace in your
hearts to the Lord.

Pray without ceasing; in *every thing*
by prayer and supplication with thanks-
giving let your request be made known to
God.   And the peace of God, which passeth all understanding, shall keep your
hearts and minds, through Christ Jesus..

Be not conformed to the world, but be
ye transformed by the renewing of your
minds.   Love not the world, neither the
things of the world.   If any man love
the world, the love of the Father is not
in him.   No man can serve two masters,
for either he will hate the one and love
the other, or else he will hold to the one
and despise the other.   Ye cannot serve
God and mammon.

In all things show thyself a pattern of
good works, that he that is of a contrary
part may be ashamed, having no evil
thing to say of you.   Be not wise in your

own conceits, for God resisteth the proud, but giveth grace to the humble. Be kindly affectioned one to another, with brotherly love; in honor preferring one another. Be not desirous of vain-glory, provoking one another, envying one another. Be rich in good works, ready to distribute, willing to communicate.

Let your *conversation* be as becometh the gospel of Christ. Let no corrupt communication proceed out of your mouth; neither foolish talking nor jesting. Every idle word that men shall speak, they shall give account thereof at the day of judgment. Speak evil of no man; let your speech be always with grace, that ye may know how to answer every man. Bear ye one another's burdens; have compassion one of another; be pitiful, be courteous.

Let us lay aside every weight and the sin which doth so easily beset us, and let us run with patience the race that is set before us; looking unto Jesus, the author and finisher of our faith, who for the joy that was set before him endured the cross, despising the shame, and is set down at the right hand of the throne of God. Despise not the chastening of the Lord, neither faint when thou art rebuked of him; for whom the Lord loveth, he chasteneth, and scourgeth every son whom he receiveth. For our light affliction, which is but for a moment, worketh for us a far more exceeding and eternal weight of glory.

Therefore, dearly beloved, our joy and our crown, so stand fast in the Lord, our dearly beloved. For now we live, if ye stand fast in the Lord.

Unto him that is able to keep you from falling, and to present you faultless before the presence of his glory with exceeding joy—to the only wise God our Saviour, be glory and majesty, dominion and power, both now and for ever. Amen.

OTHER SOLID GROUND TITLES

We recently celebrated our seventh anniversary of uncovering buried treasure to the glory of God. During these seven years we have produced nearly 200 volumes. A sample is listed below:

Biblical & Theological Studies: *Addresses to Commemorate the 100th Anniversary of Princeton Theological Seminary in 1912* by Allis, Machen, Wilson, Vos, Warfield and many more.

Notes on Galatians by J. Gresham Machen

The Origin of Paul's Religion by J. Gresham Machen

A Scientific Investigation of the Old Testament by R.D. Wilson

Theology on Fire: *Sermons from Joseph A. Alexander*

Evangelical Truth: *Sermons for the Family* by Archibald Alexander

A Shepherd's Heart: *Pastoral Sermons of James W. Alexander*

Grace & Glory: *Sermons from Princeton Chapel* by Geerhardus Vos

The Lord of Glory by Benjamin B. Warfield

The Person & Work of the Holy Spirit by Benjamin B. Warfield

The Power of God unto Salvation by Benjamin B. Warfield

Calvin Memorial Addresses by Warfield, Johnson, Orr, Webb...

The Five Points of Calvinism by Robert Lewis Dabney

Annals of the American Presbyterian Pulpit by W.B. Sprague

The Word & Prayer: *Classic Devotions from the Pen of John Calvin*

A Body of Divinity: *Sum and Substance of Christian Doctrine* by Ussher

The Collected Works of James H. Thornwell

A Puritan New Testament Commentary by John Trapp

Exposition of the Epistle to the Hebrews by William Gouge

Exposition of the Epistle of Jude by William Jenkyn

Lectures on the Book of Esther by Thomas M'Crie

Lectures on the Book of Acts by John Dick

To order any of our titles please contact us in one of three ways:

Call us at **1-866-789-7423**
Email us at **sgcb@charter.net**
Visit our website at **www.solid-ground-books.com**